1

Japanese Beetles & Grubs

Trap, Spray, & Control Them

Easy~Growing Gardening Series Vol. 8

Rosefiend Cordell

Rosefiend Publishing.

Sign up for my newsletter and get a free book! Visit me at melindacordell.com

Table of Contents

A Japanese beetle making itself at home on your flowers

FIGURE 2.—The Japanese beetle. × 3

INTRODUCTION

You know what's crazy? Fifteen years ago, I used to be in complete charge of a rose garden with over 300 roses in it, and I didn't know what a Japanese beetle looked like.

This is true. But it's simply because we didn't have Japanese beetles in my part of Missouri at that time. Can you imagine that? Occasionally I'd see a shiny green beetle on a rose blossom, but only rarely. I don't even know if I squished any, but it was highly doubtful. My main contentions were trying to get all the roses fertilized and watered, and at the time I was mainly vigilant about rose rosette disease.

At least I didn't have to contend with Japanese beetles AND rose rosette disease at the time. That would have been a mess.

In 2008, I went to St. Paul, Minnesota to summer residencies to get my MFA in writing. Only then did I understand what Japanese beetles were. I was aghast! The Hamline University campus is gorgeous, with a variety of neat little trees and shrubs and flowers that I admired greatly. On one side of the campus, next to the music building, they had a bunch of rugosa and landscape roses. Every time I passed them on the way to a workshop or class or a reading, I'd see the lovely rose blossoms covered with masses of shiny green and bronze beetles. *Masses* of them, crawling all over each other and eating their way through the satiny rose petals and the leaves. I always stopped to grab beetles off the rose blossoms and smash them. Oh, I hated them! "Thank goodness we don't have these in Missouri," I said.

Well.

Last year, we got a bunch of them.

And this year … ye gods. The Japanese beetles have extended their evil empire into my state.

If you, too, are being absolutely besieged by Japanese beetles, this book will give you ways to fight these invading hordes, in ways that those who have full-time jobs and children can manage.

Before we go into battle, though, note that fighting Japanese beetles can, in some places, be an endless task. These beetles are highly mobile, flying from place to place.

They don't blacken the sky the way the grasshopper hordes did, back in the old days. However, they still do a number on your apple and peach trees, and on your roses, and your linden trees, and a number of other plants. The control methods in this book should help mitigate the damage, and some of these may be enough to help rescue your poor plants from the worst of the damage. In some places, where the infestation is light, it might clean up the beetles altogether.

Now, when I started researching this book, most of the useful information I found was on the University Extension websites. I always recommend your local University Extension agent – there's an office in each county – but even here, I wasn't finding enough of the information I was looking for. What I wanted was a full dossier of the Japanese beetle and their habits.

As a horticulturist (and a gal who got an A in her Entomology class when she was in college), I learned several important rules in dealing with diseases and bug infestations.

1)   Know thy enemy. If you want to do an effective job in bug control, you have to get a positive ID of the pest, and then you have to know its habits, you have a better chance of stopping the infestation in its tracks.

So, if you have a problem with the spotted cucumber beetles, then you know you can find it on your squash, zucchini, and cucumber plants – and also in the blossoms of your white and yellow roses, eating the middles out of them so all the petals drop off. If you have both kinds of plants in your yard, you can spray the beetles in the garden AND spray them in your rose blossoms. Otherwise, you have a whole bunch of beetles hanging out on your roses while you're spraying in the garden – and then they come back and reinfest the cucurbits you just cleaned up.

Another example is squash bugs. If you know that the eggs look like a raft of little red eggs, you can find them on the bottoms of squash leaves, you can go on scouting missions and squash every raft. You also know when the squash bugs will be flying – so, just before they emerge, you can clear all the leafy mulch out from under your plants (some might be hiding in there) and wrap your cucurbits in floating row covers nice and tight so no squash bugs can crawl in. Then, once the flowers open, you take off the floating row covers so the pollinators can get in.

Knowing the lifecycles of the insect, where they live, and how they act, allows you to keep your plants clean with a minimum of effort.

2)   Fight the war on several fronts. So with squash bugs, you're using row covers, and squashing eggs, and if you see an adult, you squash that with your fingers. Attacking insects with chemicals only doesn't do the trick. I've sprayed bugs with insecticides until they were dripping, and still they survived! So I went in and squashed them with my fingers, and only then was I able to stop the

infestation.

Attack an infestation in several different ways. This book should give you the tools to do that.

I didn't see any other books on the market for this pest, but I did find older books written by the Agricultural Research Service of the U.S. Department of Agriculture that were just what the doctor ordered. They cited scientific research, described specific aspects of the Japanese beetle's habits, and they went into a great deal of depth about what has been done to stop the spread of the beetle ever since it appeared in the Henry A. Dreer nursery in New Jersey in 1916.

A lot of the old control methods involved chemicals such as Paris Green, arsenate of lead, and DDT. Obviously, DDT has been banned by the EPA, as well as chemicals that contain arsenic and cyanide as main ingredients. (Though it wouldn't surprise me if the current EPA brought all these chemicals back out of sheer maliciousness.) For obvious reasons, I've left these chemicals out of my book.

But these old manuals have explained a lot, and have gone through a lot of control methods. I do mean a lot. Some were methods to sanitize nursery stock from beetles and grubs, such as ultraviolet light and fumigants, that aren't feasible for the homeowner.

However, I read about a high-voltage beetle killer, also not feasible for the homeowner, which I included in this book, simply because scientists were zapping beetles with 20,000 volts of electricity and creating breathtakingly gigantic piles of dead beetles. If that isn't satisfying scientific nerdiness taken to the nth extreme, I don't know what is.

I've gone through these old records of scientific inquiry; I've looked up new research; I have gone through all kinds of home remedies and compared them to scientific studies to see what works and what doesn't.

In short, in this book I have compiled as many weapons for your Japanese beetle arsenal as possible, where these weapons can be effectively used in the beetle's life cycle, and how they can be deployed.

The Japanese beetle likely won't be eradicated. Great entomological minds have been working on this problem for a solid century now, using extremely lethal chemicals and other means to try and stop the infestation, and they were doing this way back in the days when Japanese beetle numbers were far, far smaller than they are now.

However, there are ways that we can mitigate the damage the beetles do, and you might be able to bring down the scores of unwanted visitors to your roses, and kill off a number of the unwanted residents in your lawn.

I hope to do this in a way that's interesting and amusing for you to read, because if there's anything I hate, it's the idea of my readers falling into a coma halfway through a paragraph. So I'll do my best to keep that from happening. It's only fair.

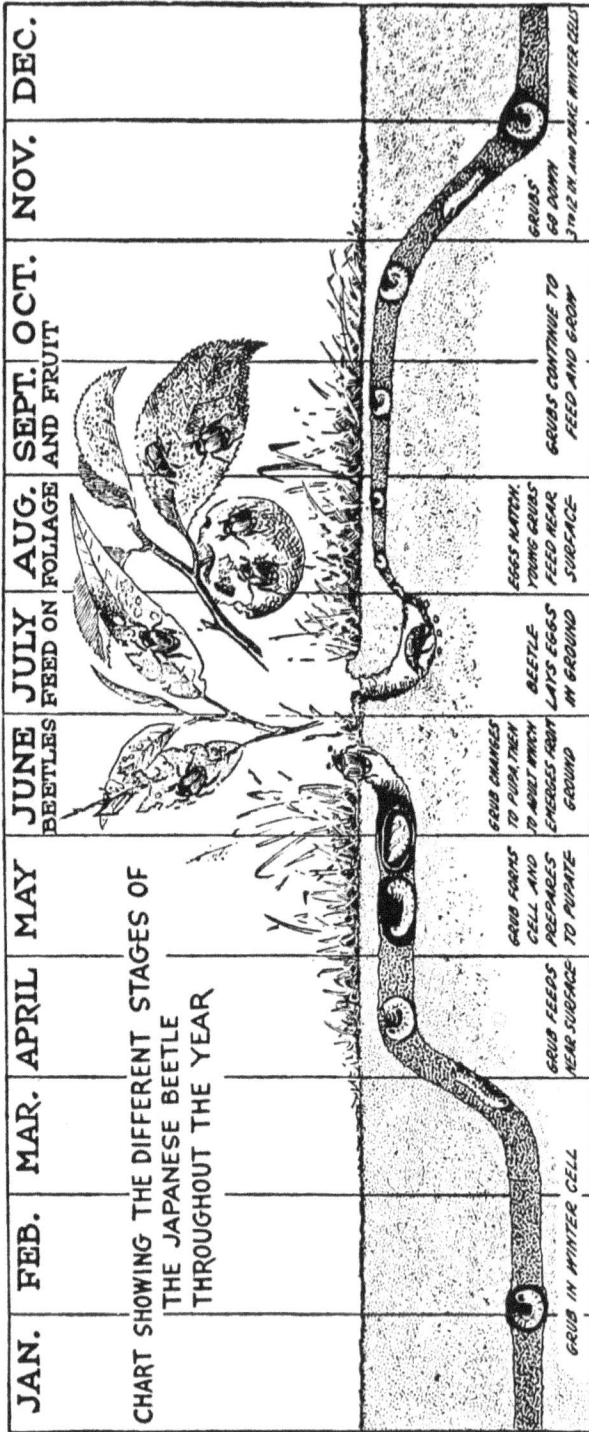

JAN.	FEB.	MAR.	APRIL	MAY	JUNE BEETLES	JULY FEED ON FOLIAGE	AUG.	SEPT. AND FRUIT	OCT.	NOV.	DEC.

CHART SHOWING THE DIFFERENT STAGES OF
THE JAPANESE BEETLE
THROUGHOUT THE YEAR

GRUB IN WINTER CELL

GRUB FEEDS NEAR SURFACE

GRUB FORMS CELL AND PREPARES TO PUPATE

GRUB CHANGES TO PUPA THEN TO ADULT WHICH EMERGES FROM GROUND

BEETLE LAYS EGGS IN GROUND

EGGS HATCH. YOUNG GRUBS FEED NEAR SURFACE

GRUBS CONTINUE TO FEED AND GROW

GRUBS GO DOWN 3 TO 12 IN AND MAKE WINTER CELL

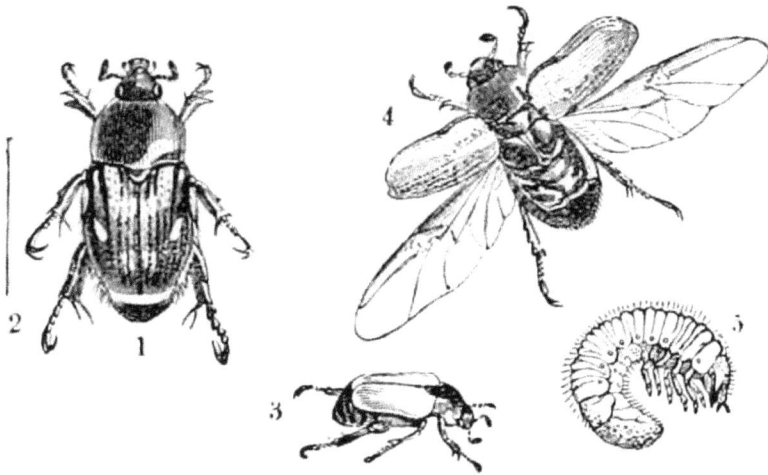

Japanese beetles and grub.

KNOW THY ENEMY

Description

Japanese beetles (*Popillia japonica*) are about the size of a dime, about a 1/2 to 3/4 inch long. They sport an iridescent copper shell with a green head, with six tufts of white hair along their sides under the edges of their wing shells. They're actually quite a pretty insect when they aren't attacking your roses and apples en masse.

History

In August 1916, two inspectors from the New Jersey Department of Agriculture were at the Henry A. Dreer nursery near Riverton, N.J., inspecting plants for unknown diseases or insects (as they do). They collected a dozen

13

unknown beetles on that visit, so they checked the insect collections at the National Museum in Washington, D.C. There they found that the specimens were Japanese beetles. At this time, the beetles occurred only on the main islands of Japan – Honsu, Kyushu, Shikoku, and Hokkaido.

It's not known for sure how the beetles arrived on American soil – they're thought to have arrived in a shipment of *Iris kaempferi* (known now as *Iris ensata*), a popular garden plant at that time. (The Japanese iris is still a nice, low-maintenance perennial.)

In Japan, the beetle was not a garden pest. The main islands at the time were heavily forested mountainous country, conditions that didn't allow the beetle to do very well. Furthermore, due to the cool weather in the Japanese islands that the beetle lived in, the beetle had a two-year life cycle, so it didn't reproduce rapidly. Habitat for the beetle's larvae (the grubs) was also scarce in Japan. The nation does have grasslands on Hokkaido, but they also contain a host of natural predators that keep the beetle numbers down.

However, when the beetle showed up in America, those checks and balances didn't exist.

Warm weather that allows it to move through a complete life cycle in one year –

No natural enemies to keep it in check –

A ton of habitat for its grubs, in the form of everlasting lawns –

300 species of plants serving as a veritable all-you-can-eat buffet –

This country is a veritable paradise for that beetle.

The Japanese beetle hit America and flourished. In very little time, the beetle spread through the East and clear out to the Mississippi.

Entomologists had already recognized its destructive potential and had jumped into action. The year after it was discovered, in 1917, the Japanese Beetle Laboratory was established in New Jersey to study these insects and try to slow its spread.

Every year sees a new area added to its range – as gardeners in Missouri and other areas have recently seen.

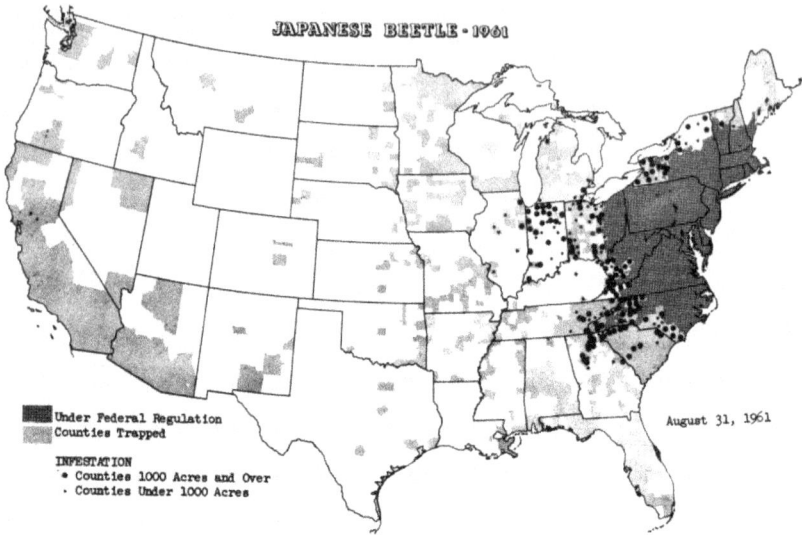

A map of Japanese beetle coverage in the nation in 1961.

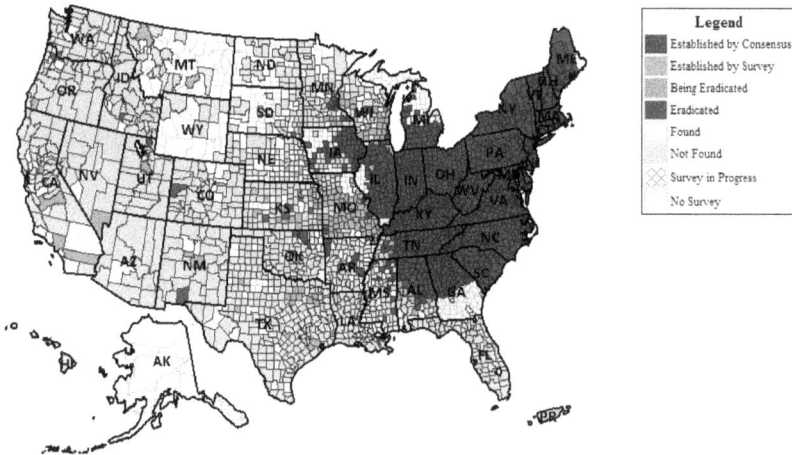

*Current Survey Map Of Japanese Beetle Distribution,
from PestTracker*

A note on Japanese Beetle habits

A good tactician understands that, when you have the resources for it, a war should be fought on more than one front. Each front should target your enemy's weak spots. You just keep hitting and moving, hitting and moving, until you have won the battle or have routed your enemy. And always stay one step ahead of your enemy.

These tactics, though greatly simplified, also apply to fighting diseases and pests in the garden and in the field. **With Japanese beetles, several different methods of control are necessary for the most effective knock-down of these noxious pests.**

These tactics include understanding the habits and life cycle of the Japanese beetle.

Knowing what an insect needs to live is key to good control. Then you can target all of these things to kill off a large infestation.

Habits and lifecycle

A Japanese beetle's life usually starts on some hot July night, when a female Japanese beetle that has been chomping up apples and leaves and rose blossoms flies down to the grass, works her way down through the grass to the soil. There she will dig a little burrow two or three inches deep and lay a little cluster of eggs. The next morning, she crawls to the surface to fly back up into the trees, find another mate, and eat a thousand more leaves, and the next night she'll lay more eggs in a little burrow.

These eggs will eventually turn into approximately five million grubs ... actually, that's not true. Each female lays about 40 to 60 eggs – still more than enough. There's nothing I hate more than an overachieving beetle.

The Japanese beetles themselves die off by the middle of August, but the eggs are still there, as are the grubs, busily hatching and growing underground.

The eggs absorb water in order to grow, then hatch in midsummer, about mid-July. The grubs, or larvae, emerge an inch or two underground, where they begin to feed on grass roots. These white grubs are an inch long when fully grown and rest in a C shape. When you turn over the soil in your garden, you'll probably find a couple of grubs there in your shovelful of dirt, though some of those grubs might also be for June bugs, chafers, or some other grub from the Scarab family of beetles.

It's harder to tell Japanese beetle grubs from those of June bugs and other related beetles, because the grubs are generally differentiated by the pattern of hairs on their hind ends. Entomology is fun! No, seriously, it really is.

During summer, when the ground is warm, the grubs inhabit the top two inches of the ground, feeding on grass roots. By September, these grubs are almost an inch long. In late fall, the cold weather will drive the grubs deeper into the soil. They'll dig about four to eight inches down and hibernate there through the winter, safe from the worst of the cold.

In spring, the grubs return to the grass roots to feed until they're plump. In late spring, the grubs pupate, metamorphose into beetles, and pop up out of the soil for their late-spring and early-summer buffet of destruction. And, of course, mating. I was going to say "mating like rabbits," but rabbits ain't got nothing on these little hedonists.

It's important to note that newly-laid Japanese beetle eggs and newly-hatched grubs need enough rain to keep from drying out. Years with bad droughts can put a dent in the grub population by destroying the eggs, because the eggs must absorb water in order to allow the embryo beetle to develop.

If your lawn is having trouble with grubs, and if you're able to do this, stop watering your lawn from June to mid-July, in order to help kill off Japanese beetle eggs. This is probably a good reason to grow drought-tolerant turfgrasses in your lawn.

The grubs themselves are more resistant to dry soil. The grubs usually go through three instars (that is, growing periods that end with a molt of their skin as they grow too big for it); during each instar, the grub can withstand a huge loss of water in its body. During the first instar, right after they hatch, these grubs can lose up to 44 percent water before they croak.

If the soil temperature drops to -9.4 degrees Celsius, or 15 degrees Fahrenheit, nearly 100 percent of the grubs will die. But this has got to be the soil temperature, not just the air temperature. This drop of soil temperature can be brought on by sudden, extreme changes in the air temperature, and no snow cover. (A blanket of snow insulates the soil against these drastic, grub-killing drops – too bad.)

Also, freezing rain causes the water in the soil to freeze, stabbing many grubs with ice crystals. So there is that.

A very dry summer or a terrible freezing winter causes a drop in the local population, but adequate rainfall and favorable temperatures can cause a spike in the numbers of beetles the next year.

An additional note: Beetles are very alkaline creatures, but they have a very broad tolerance to soil pH, so acidic soils don't seem to bother the grubs at all. Also too bad.

What attracts Japanese beetles?

The answer to this is straightforward: food and sex.

Japanese beetles find food by following certain chemical odors in the air. They find love, or whatever, through following pheromones in the air. And the more pheromones there are in the air, the more beetles there are in an area, all of which are going at it. Beetles will fly long distances to find these party trees, as you've probably noticed when you go outside and find your apple tree dripping with mating beetles.

Love is in the air

Male beetles will fly to plants where females were feeding, or pretty much anyplace where the females are. In the morning, when the females climb out of the holes they've dug to lay their eggs, a bunch of males will fly over and land and try to mate with her. And she's like, "Dudes, I just woke up, geez." An entomologist noted that males always approached a female against the wind, and when the wind shifted, they would change their path to follow the trail of pheromones coming off her.

So if a couple of beetles are on a plant, you can bet they'll soon be joined by six hundred more.

Note: this is a good reason to start killing the beetles as soon as they start showing up. If you can bring their numbers down right at the start, they will have a harder time infesting the plants in your yard.

An old study found that 50 percent more beetles landed on infested foliage than on uninfested foliage. This is why beetles will flock to one plant, while a plant of the same species in the same area will be relatively clean of beetles.

Side note: I'm interested in hearing if there's been any scientific work done on blocking or masking beetle pheromones. I've heard of some people using essential oils to block or confuse the beetles, and I'm curious about how well this method would work.

The smell of food is also in the air

Certain essential oils, some fruit fragrances, and the smell of fermentation will attract the beetles. The beetles are always attracted to fruits with high sugar content.

Japanese beetles are also attracted by the smell of fermenting fruit on the ground or in the trees. Some entomologists recommend removing rotted fruit to protect the sound fruit from beetle attack.

Beetles gather in huge numbers on early apples and peaches, forming clusters in the shape of a ball, feeding until all that remains is a core or a pit. In 1940, two entomologists counted 296 beetles on one apple. The beetles also cluster in balls occasionally on foliage or blossoms.

On fruit trees, the beetles prefer fruit that's been damaged or has been infected by disease over healthy fruit. This is because it's easier for the beetles to eat their way into an apple if there's a hole in the skin, or into a peach if there's a spot of rot.

The same goes for grapes. The beetles ate grapes that were infested with grape berry moth, or those that were infected by black rot – even if the grapes were immature. Only when that food source was exhausted did the beetles move on to healthy grapes nearby.

So remember: To discourage Japanese beetles, get rid of rotting fruit, diseased fruit, or fruit with holes in it.

Japanese also attack and defoliate unhealthy trees first before moving on to healthy trees. One study noted that peach trees that were infected with the peach yellow disease and little peach disease were attacked by the beetle, while healthy trees nearby were mostly unscathed.

So be sure to keep your trees healthy. Mulch them with a layer of compost and water it in. Keep the weeds down around the tree so there's less competition between roots.

Beetles never stay long in one place, and constantly move from one plant to another. They can fly several miles in a day. One reason why beetle control is so difficult is their extreme mobility. When you kill off beetles, more beetles move in from elsewhere.

The adults feed on over 300 plant species (lately I've seen that number quoted as being 400). They chew out the tissue between the leaf veins, leaving lacy skeletons that fall from the tree. So if you see a lot of lacy leaf skeletons collecting on the ground in May or June, look up – you might see the beetles in the top branches of the tree. Beetles will start in the top foliage of trees and plants, in places that are exposed to full sun, and then work their way downward through the plants.

Note: Beetles don't like to feed in the shade, so if you have a shade garden, you're not going to see as much beetle damage.

The most feeding takes place on warm summer days when the sun is out, when the temperatures are between 83 and 95 degrees. If the relative humidity falls below 60 percent, beetles don't want to fly, so they stay in place and feed a lot instead. They also do not fly on cool, windy days, and they don't fly on rainy days.

DAMAGE CAUSED BY BEETLES AND THEIR GRUBS

Japanese beetles are one of the few insects that do a lot of damage both as a larvae *and* an adult.

The larvae feed on your lawn and grass roots, and damages hundreds of acres of turf like the possessed crazed evil nanobot it is. Then when the grub is all grown up and has metamorphosed into a beetle, it comes up out of the ground and eats everything else.

The adult beetles eat the foliage and flowers of over 300 plant species. These species include, but are not limited to, rose, mountain ash, willow, linden, elm, Virginia creeper, Japanese and Norway maples, birches, pin oaks, horse chestnut, rose of Sharon (hibiscus), sycamore, apple trees, crabapples, plum, and cherry. And cannas. And wild and cultivated grapes. And more! Items on this list will vary from region to region, naturally.

Japanese beetles can do a lot of damage to corn by eating the silk, which of course stops the kernels from forming. If you see that the silk on your corn plant is being clipped back to less than a half-inch when less than 50 percent of your corn crop has been pollinated, you have problems.

In some areas, you might be able to mitigate damage to your corn crop by delaying your corn planting. Check with your local University Extension for alternate planting dates in your area. In Missouri, corn is usually planted after May 15. If you have several later planting dates, the corn's silk might not be as developed during the beetles' peak damage period in June, and you might be able to have silk in July, when damage is tapering off. Late planting helps.

Beetles do not eat dogwood, forsythia, holly and lilac. They don't eat gingko leaves, either. In one study, beetles that were confined with gingko leaves died rather than eat them. However, when the leaves were coated with the odors that the beetles liked (one of which was eugenol, a chemical found in rose petals), the beetles ate them right up. They're attracted to the odors – that's how they find food (and mates.)

Adult beetles will turn leaves into lacy skeletons by eating all the leaf tissue and leaving the veins. An elm tree had tons of lacy brown leaves lying on the ground all around it, which the beetles had skeletonized.

Damage starts appearing in May or early June, depending on where the United States you live, as the beetles emerge from the ground.

Adults are most active from 9 to 3 p.m. on hot, sunny

days and they do most of their feeding in the tops of trees, as well as on flowers and fruit. They like eating in full sun and don't seem to like to feed in heavy shade. So if you have a shade garden, those flowers might be spared from the beetle onslaught.

What's crazy about these beetles (well, it's not so much crazy as it is crazy-making) is that you can go outside one day and look at your apple tree and think, Hey, I'm going to have a really nice harvest this year – and the next day you go out and see clumps of rabid beetles covering your fruit and leaves and eating big holes in them. Or you knock against a rose blossom and a bunch of Japanese beetles fall out. Or you walk outside wearing a shirt with roses on it and you get mobbed by beetles. (Actually, that last one hasn't happened, though I wouldn't be surprised if it does.)

Apples showing damage and extensive damage from Japanese beetles

As the Japanese beetle feeds through the month, you start seeing leaves on certain trees turn a uniform brownish color as the beetles skeletonize the leaves. I've observed this browning take place on lindens, apple trees, crabapples, sycamores, grapevines (both wild and cultivated), elms, and birches. The leaves lose some of their greenness, and then the tree gradually turns brownish as the beetles eat their way through their leaves.

The beetles die out by August, and the defoliated trees are generally able to recover.

If you have a tree that's badly damaged, give her an organic fertilizer that's low in nitrogen but has phosphorus and potassium and trace minerals. Put a layer of compost on the ground around the dripline of the tree and water it in. Lay a water hose under the branches and let it run for a while, then move it to another spot under the branches. Keep repeating until all the area around the tree has had a good, long drink. If you're having a drought, give your tree a little extra water now and then (if local regulations allow this).

Prepare for next year today.

Here's something you can do right now to get ready for next year's onslaught. **Walk around your yard and write down which plants were attacked by Japanese beetles. Look for damage in trees and large shrubs – they might have attacked some of these too, without your realizing it.**

If you have a gardening journal (I hope you have a gardening journal), put that information in there, and this winter you can put it on next year's calendar. (Note: In the back of this book I have a chapter from my vegetable gardening book about keeping a garden journal. If you do any kind of outdoor work, keep one. My gardening journal was the single most helpful thing I had when I was a city horticulturist with no full-time staff trying to put out metaphorical fires all over the city.)

Once you've made your list of affected plants, keep it ready for next year. **When spring rolls around, you know which plants you can target early in the season to control the Japanese beetles. You'll also know to start keeping an eye on them in late May for the first signs of beetles.** Write down the dates on which they appear, and on which plants. Then next year, you can put these dates on your calendar and have all the control methods loaded and ready to deploy.

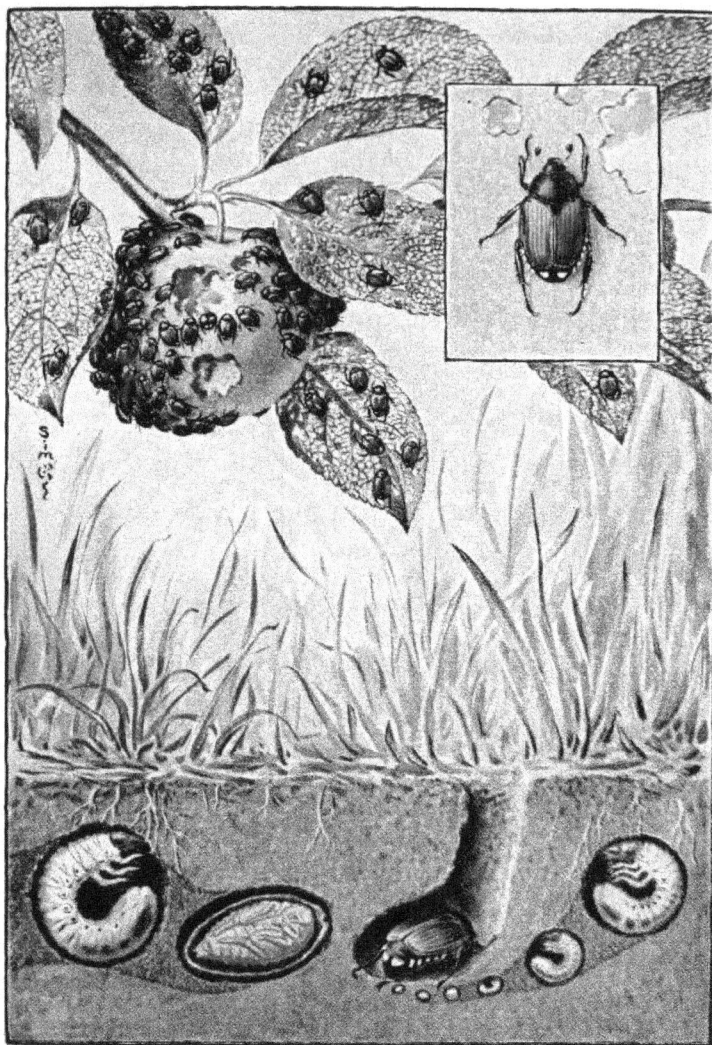

Adult beetles feeding on fruit and leaves, about one-half natural size. Insert, adult beetle, about twice natural size. Figures below ground represent seasonal history of the Japanese beetle. Left to right, mature grub (late spring); pupa; beetle laying eggs (summer); developing grubs (late summer and fall); all about twice natural size.

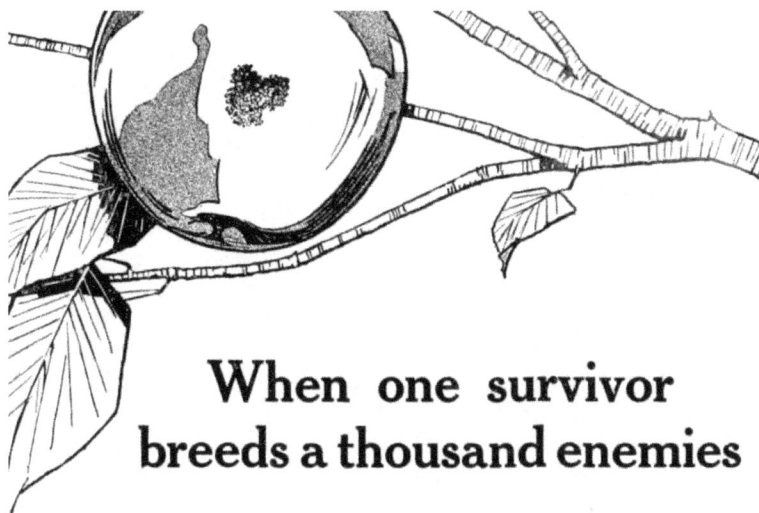

When one survivor breeds a thousand enemies

JAPANESE BEETLE LOOK-ALIKES

Good control methods also include knowing exactly what you're targeting in the lawn and in the garden. There are a number of related beetles in the Scarab family running loose all over America – though not in the same powerhouse numbers that you see in the Japanese beetles, thank goodness.

I'm including their pictures so you can be sure about what beetles are attacking your plants – and which ones you should target (the first one) and which ones you can give a free pass to (all the rest). Here are some common Scarab beetles in the United States.

Adult Japanese beetle, *Popillia japonica*

Credit: USGS Bee Inventory and Monitoring Lab

Adult false Japanese beetle, *Strigoderma arboricola*

Photo credit: Whitney Cranshaw, Colorado State University, Bugwood.org

Adult rose chafer, *Macrodactylus subspinosus*

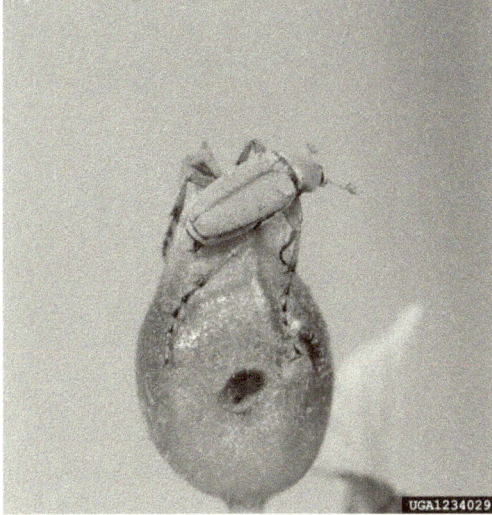

Photo credit: Clemson University – USDA Cooperative Extension
Slide Series, Bugwood.org

Adult May/June beetle, *Phyllophaga species*

Photo credit: Bruce Watt, University of Maine, Bugwood.org

Adult masked chafer, *Cyclocephala borealis*

Photo credit: Phil Sloderbeck, Kansas State University,
Bugwood.org

Adult black turfgrass Ataenius, *Ataenius spretulus*

Photo credit: Whitney Cranshaw, Colorado State University,
Bugwood.org

Adult hybrid Japanese beetle, aka green June bug,
Cotinis nitida

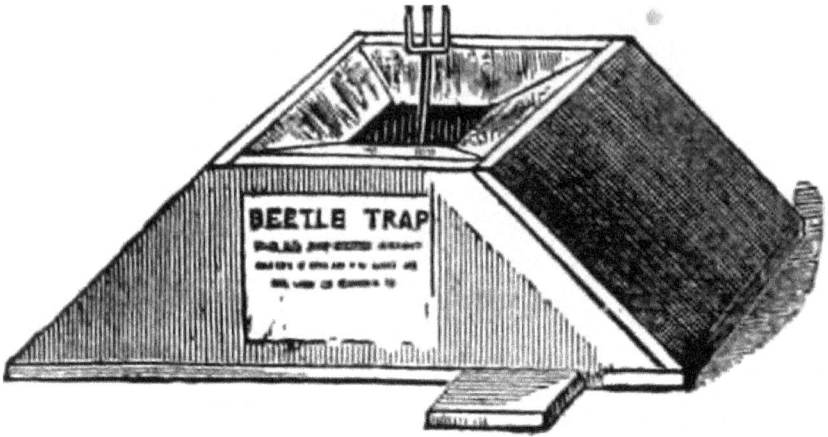

BEETLE TRAP

CONTROL OF JAPANESE BEETLES

This year, my roses at home were swarmed by Japanese beetles, both on the blossoms and on the leaves. The beetles were thick, almost as thick as I saw them up in Minnesota. I found over ten Japanese beetles on one rosebud that hadn't opened yet. Actually, ten was all I could manage to count. I grabbed a handful off the rosebud and kept opening and closing my hand to count them, but they kept milling around and flying away. The whole time I was doing this, there were scores of beetles flying off the plant. The jerks.

When I was at home, I tried to grab as many beetles as I could off my roses so I could feed them to the chickens, but the beetles would bite the skin on my hands. The chickens, in their hurry to grab the beetles, would nip my hands with their beaks. And, quite often, the beetles would fly away before I could grab them. Catching the beetles is tricky, because when you go after a Japanese beetle, they do one of several things.

1) They simply fall off the plant. Many times, if you see a beetle with its hind legs sticking up in the air, that means they're going to drop as soon as you touch them.

2) The beetles fly away quicker than anything.

3) In some instances, the beetles will hold on very tightly to the leaf you're trying to pull them off of.

I quickly came up with the idea of knocking the beetles into a small cup of water that had a little water in it. I used a large, lightweight measuring cup with a handle, because it had a big opening for the beetles to fall into, and was easy to hold under a branch. Beetles just fall into the water, where they can't fly or crawl, but just float with their legs waving around. They'd grab other beetles, and pretty soon there'd be a raft of helpless beetles in the water.

If you're not feeding these beetles to your chickens, add a few drops of dish detergent to the water. The detergent will make the water more "wet" by lowering its surface tension. As a result, the beetles will die faster because the detergent allows the water to get into their spiracles (breathing tubes) much more quickly.

One afternoon I looked out the back door and realized

that the top of my apple tree had turned brown. What had happened? "Tent caterpillars?" I asked aloud. But no, it was too early in the year to be tent caterpillars, and the damage was wrong, too. Tent caterpillar damage tends to be localized in small areas around the tree. This damage was evenly spread through all the top branches of the tree, browning the leaves evenly. So I went out and looked at the leaves, and damned if I didn't see a crapload of Japanese beetles busily munching away. When I shook the tree, a cloud of Japanese beetles fell and buzzed all around me like something out of Hitchcock's *Birds*. I didn't feel any need to shake the tree again after that.

So Japanese beetles weren't exclusively a pest to roses. Then I started noticing Japanese beetle damage everywhere. They targeted all kinds of trees – crabapples, linden, elms, goldenrain trees, and peach trees – as well as grapevines and many other plants. They seemed to target a lot of plants in the rose family. (Then again, *everything* seems to target plants in the rose family.)

I ended up making it an evening routine to walk around my backyard knocking Japanese beetles in a cup with a little water at the bottom. I'd hunt through my rosebushes, then the multiflora rose, then the elm trees, and then my apple trees for those beetles. While I was hunting beetles in the rosebush, Henny Penny would come over and stand on top of my shoe while I worked. Then I'd give her some beetles. It was very comfortable and friendly. She's a good little hen.

Sometimes I'd see the Japanese beetles swarming all over one of my apples, eating their way into the fruit. When I picked the fruit and dropped it into my cup of water, beetle after beetle would start coming out of the inside of the apple, like clowns squeezing out of a clown car. It was nuts.

The kids had brought a sled out into the backyard, because my daughter wanted to put soap on the Slip and Slide and see if they could slide down it with the sled. (It didn't work, but I think it would have worked if we'd had a slope.) The sled was still outside because apparently putting things away is a Mom chore.

Anyway, I put the sled by the apple tree and filled it with water. Then I put about an inch of water in a big, lightweight cup. I'd walk around the apple tree and knock Japanese beetles into the cup. Then I would call the chickies and pour the water and beetles into the water-filled sled. The girls would pluck the beetles out of the water and eat them, snap! Snap! Snap! It's a good sound. Most (not all) chickens love these beetles, and I felt fortunate that I could kill off these pests and give my chickies a treat.

Sprays and Dusts

Here are some chemical and organic insecticides to spray against beetles. Whichever kind you use, always read and follow label directions. Don't spray these insecticides on windy days, or when bees are out and about. (Bees have a bad enough time as it is.) If you are spraying a food crop, note the number of days you need to leave between the last spraying and date of harvest.

Something to remember: Many of the insecticides I mention here will be able to knock down Japanese beetles. However, you'll have to keep repeating applications about twice a week – every three to four days – because new beetles will keep migrating in every day.

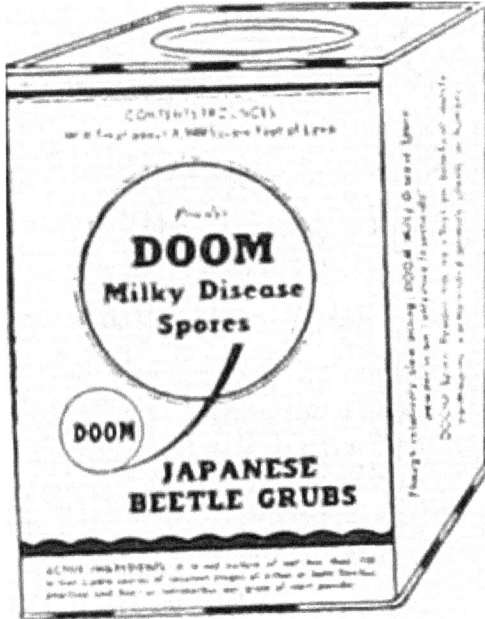

Chemical insecticides

I don't generally list insecticides, because it's impossible to say which will be on the market after five years and which won't. As a matter of fact, I had to rewrite half my rose book because I got through a full draft before I discovered that lime sulfur, which was a good, low-toxic fungicide, had been banned by the EPA. I had used it extensively in the rose garden when I was city horticulturist, but things change through the years! So, keep that in mind when you sally forth to the chemicals aisle at your local nursery.

A second reason that I don't often list chemicals is that I prefer to find organic solutions to insect problems. Even when you're careful when you spray, there's no real good way to know how long these linger in the soil, affecting the beneficial insects that you want to keep alive.

On an additional note, remember that chemical insecticides are not only toxic to Japanese beetles, but to honeybees as well. Honeybees are having a very rough time due to large numbers of dieoff in hives. They're still plagued by the varroa mite, which kills many honeybees. The indiscriminate use of pesticides is also to blame for their decline.

Quick tips to help keep honeybees safe while you're spraying for Japanese beetles (courtesy of the University of Tennessee Extension):

Don't spray insecticides while honeybees are foraging in the blossoms of those plants

Mow off any clover or dandelion flowers under the trees that you're spraying.

Sprays are actually more friendly to bees (though I use the term "friendly" loosely) than dusts. Bees are safer (mostly) once the sprays dry, but dust stays out longer and affects them.

Don't spray near honey bee colonies.

Try to use insecticides that are less toxic to honeybees.

Cabaryl, sold as Sevin, is another insecticide that's

effective against Japanese beetles. This insecticide will reduce damage for about two weeks. However, it is toxic to bees and other helpful insects.

Some say that liquid Sevin might be a better choice, because after it's dried, bees won't bring it back to the hive, but it still kills the beetles in its dried form.

Malathion, also toxic to honeybees, has a bad odor when you spray it, so you might skip spraying it in public places.

Pyrethroids like permethrin, deltamethrin, difenthrin, and cyfluthrin, are also effective. Some of these formulations may be Restricted Use Pesticides, which means you can't use them without a license. Many of these, however, are available to the homeowner.

These synthetic pyrethroids generally provide about 2 to 3 weeks of protection for your plant foliage, though, so you won't have to apply these as often. Nineteen days of effective protection seems to be the norm, even in plants that received frequent and heavy rains.

Please use all of these with care. They are very toxic to humans, animals, birds, and fish. It's a good idea to wear a mask while spraying. Even when I'd be spraying chemical controls back in my horticulture days, sometimes I'd get a noseful of the chemical, even though I was always very careful. Be sure to take care of yourselves, and others.

Systemic insecticides

Systemic insecticides are non-organic poisons that are absorbed into the plant's system where it kills insects that eat on it.

Somebody asked me if a systemic insecticide would work against Japanese beetles. They do, to a certain extent. Landscaping companies using systemics in the field have reported decent results.

As with any control method, systemic insecticides have limitations. For obvious reasons, you shouldn't use a systemic insecticide on a fruit tree, unless you want to grow poisoned apples for Snow White. (Protip: Don't.) Also, systemics take a little while to travel through the plant, so you'll need to be sure to apply them a month or two before the Japanese beetles show up.

HOWEVER, systemic insecticides will affect butterflies, honeybees, and other pollinators if the plant is flowering after it's had the systemic insecticide applied. If you have roses, put the systemic down a month or two before May, when the Japanese beetles emerge and start chomping on everything. Add new systemic every month. That should give your plant some measure of protection – and if the Japanese beetles still eat your roses, at least you're getting to kill them off in return.

Organic insecticides

I prefer to use organics, which are less harmful to humans and the environment, but they still will knock beetles down very nicely.

Pyrethrin, an old favorite of organic gardeners, is an insecticide made from daisies. **Pyola** – basically pyrethrin mixed with canola oil – is the same stuff, only with an extra beetle-killing kick, due to the canola oil. Pyola provides about five days of protection against beetles. And the really nice thing about pyola is that you can use it on your food plants (raspberries, blueberries, etc.) up until the day of harvest. This insecticide also stays put even after a rainstorm, *if* you give it time to dry on the plant before the rain starts.

Pyola seems to be the most effective organic product against beetles. This insecticide uses two modes of action to kill beetles. Beetles to some degree can build up a resistance against the pyrethrum itself, but the oil is a different story.

Beetles (and this is true about insects in general) breathe differently than birds and mammals. In their abdomen around their sides are small openings called spiracles. Beetles breathe like an accordion – they expand their thorax, air comes in; they collapse it, air is pressed out. The oxygen passes into their bodies through these tubes and is absorbed directly into the insects' blood. So that's how the respiration process works for beetles.

Now, beetles are water-resistant, as their exoskeleton is waxy, and they have all those tiny hairs on their bodies to keep water out. But oil is a different matter – because oil will clog up the spiracles right away. The beetle can't breathe, and pretty soon it croaks.

Pyola also serves as a feeding deterrent, and also gives rapid knockdown. Some beetles will recover from knockdown, but the canola oil causes them die later.

Insecticides with oil added shouldn't be sprayed when temperatures are over 90 degrees. Don't go adding a lot of oil to your pesticides, as too much oil on leaves can burn them.

A side note that I found amusing, or something: While reading about canola oils, I found a lot of random blogs all in a panic because they claimed that canola oil will kill you! "One has to ask if God created a plant to be poisonous is it correct to think that man can change this just through some ability of his own?" Yes, dear, because God also gave us the ability to use our minds in powerful ways, as well as the ability to use scientific principles wisely, bless his heart.

The human mind is a wonderful, wonderful thing – when we use it with common sense. Moving on.

Neem oil (azadirachtin) is moderately effective against Japanese beetles. Neem oil products generally protect the plant for only two days. This doesn't kill beetles as much as it causes them to not want to eat your plants – which is also acceptable. Neem oil is more easily washed off by rain, however.

Insecticidal soap, and extracts of garlic, orange peels, or hot peppers are generally ineffective.

Spinosad (A & D) is an organic substance made by a soil bacterium that is used in insect control. It affects the nervous system of the insects that eat or touch it, causing their muscles to flex uncontrollably, and they die within a day or two. It doesn't seem to affect the Japanese beetle as well as some other insecticides, though.

Note: Even some of the organic insecticides can make some of the users dizzy and light-headed, so always spray carefully, and wash up when you're done using them. Just because it's organic doesn't mean it's harmless. You can find plenty of harmful substances in nature, after all, such as poisonous mushrooms and arsenic. They're organic too! But this doesn't mean you put them in your soup! So, as with any insecticide, be sure to wash your hands with soap and water when you're done using it, and handle it with care when you're using it.

Lead arsenate and DDT
Yeah, just … don't use these.

Natural plant extracts
Some of these severely burned the leaves of plants. Test on one or two plants before you spray the garden with them.

Barriers
Kaolin clay (Surround) is coming into use more and more. It's a non-toxic barrier made up of kaolin clay, which is used as an anti-caking agent in processed foods, and also is used in toothpaste, Kaopectate, and kitty litter.

Basically, kaolin clay white-washes the plant in a fine film of microscopic clay particles. It doesn't always deter the beetles from eating the foliage.

Kaolin clay does have promise for fruit trees, because the clay can be washed from the fruit after they've been harvested. Kaolin clay doesn't look very attractive on the plants once they've been sprayed, but it seems to protect plum and cherry trees against the beetles.

Hydrated lime

Hydrated lime was said to be moderately toxic to larvae in the ground. Some rose growers ages ago said that hydrated lime added to the soil killed off grubs in the soil. However, scientific tests seem to indicate that adding hydrated lime to the soil doesn't seem to have much of an effect on the number of grubs in the soil. Adult beetles seem to avoid freshly limed grass, but once the dew falls and washes away the effects of the lime, they're back to laying eggs in that section of turf again.

However, **hydrated lime** as a spray works pretty well. It's non-poisonous and acts as a repellent. In the old days, you'd mix 1 pound of hydrated lime and a quarter-pound of aluminum sulfate with 5 gallons of water. These days, you can buy hydrated lime at the store. This spray leaves a very white residue on the plants, and the adult beetles mostly leave the plants alone after they've been sprayed.

When you're spraying hydrated lime, keep shaking the sprayer to keep the lime from settling to the bottom of the container.

Diatomaceous earth

DE is an inert, fine white dust that, like chalk, is made up of diatoms – a single-celled algae with sharp-edged shells made of silicon dioxide.

Insects have an exoskeleton, a hard outer shell, that keeps their interior moisture inside. DE does two things to that exterior shell. First, the microscopically sharp edges of the diatoms cut into the exoskeleton. Second, the DE absorbs the water-protecting oils and fats from the exoskeleton's outer layer. Result? The insect dries out and croaks.

Fun fact – You know how I said chalk has diatoms the way that DE does? When my daughter drew pictures on the sidewalk with chalk, slugs would crawl across the chalk lines and explode, due to the diatoms in the chalk cutting through their protective slime layer. So I'd go outside in the morning and see exploded slug remains next to a chalk line. This will ruin your breakfast.

DE won't cause instant knock-down of your beetles, but the beetles (and other insects) that come in contact with this dust should eventually dry out and die, especially if the summer is dry.

If you dust your plant's leaves with DE, do wear a dust mask, as the dust is not only abrasive to insects, but also to your lungs.

If it rains, you have to reapply it, as DE loses its effectiveness when wet.

Trapping and Squishing

Hand collection

Hand collection is the organic way to kill beetles, though it's slow. It's straightforward – **knock the beetles of the plant into a cup of soapy water with a little bit of rubbing alcohol, or kerosene.** (I used rubbing alcohol in entomology class to kill bugs for my collection, and it's a very effective bug killer.)

When you're collecting beetles by hand, you have to

move fast. When disturbed, the beetles fold their legs and drop to the ground before you can grab them.

I noticed that when I went around the yard every evening cleaning up beetles, soon I didn't see as many in the yard. Fewer beetles in the yard mean that there were fewer beetle pheromones calling other beetles. **So even cutting the numbers of beetles means having fewer incoming beetles, and less damage.** Every little bit helps.

In August, the numbers of beetles starts declining. I found them on the blossoms of the bindweeds, mostly, and the roses, but no longer in huge number as before. And after a while, once the eggs are laid in the grass, the beetles die off (though their newly hatched grubs are quite alive in the soil – darn 'em).

Protip: If you can't stand squishing Japanese beetles with your hands or with dishwashing gloves (they'll squirt out of your fingers with those), use a pair of pliers to squish them. Pliers will let you pick those beetles out of the blooms of your roses without shattering the blossoms.

Jarring

The name is a little confusing, but basically this is when you go out in the morning, probably before seven a.m. while it's still cool outside, lay a couple of sheets flat on the ground under a tree, **then shake the tree hard so the beetles fall out onto the sheets.** The beetles will be too cold to fly off. You then gather up the beetles and dump them in a bucket of soapy water to kill them.

If you have a lot of beetles, dump their remains in your compost pile and cover them up. You can compost the beetles that way, getting some good organic matter for your soil, while also keeping the dead beetles from smelling up the place. It's beetle burial with benefits.

Trapping

The traps sold for beetle (adult) control use either a female sex pheromone (a "come hither" pheromone), or a "floral-base lure" (that is, some of the floral-based or a food-based chemical smell) to lure in beetles. However, a lot of beetles come into the area, lured by the smell, but then end up on a nearby plant instead, chewing it to shreds.

These traps really attract a lot of beetles – but many of them do not actually get into the bag. Instead, they fly around the bag in huge numbers, and there's this serious 1960s love fest happening all over the outside of the bag.

One way to deal with this is to occasionally **spray around the bag with organic insecticide** and knock the flying beetles out of the air ... into oblivion.

Or, to keep them out of your yard, put the bags in your neighbor's yard a half-mile away.

Kidding!

However, if you have a lot of property, like a pasture, you can put a couple of traps way out there and lure the beetles away from your yard. In these cases, set up the bags a quarter-mile away from susceptible plantings.

These traps do help in several respects. If the infestation is light, these traps really do help. They also capture females before they're finished laying eggs, which helps to keep local infestations at a minimum.

Near houses surrounded with trees, these traps will probably draw beetles only from the immediate surroundings, since the buildings, trees, and shrubs will slow down the air currents that would otherwise spread the pheromone far and wide. So if you have a place out of the wind, the traps actually will help trap the beetles in your yard without bringing more in.

Naturally, open fields and wide yards are another story,

as air currents can travel freely and bring beetles in from 500 yards away.

The best use for traps would be in a large, cooperative campaign over a large area. **If a single city pushed for residents to put up beetle traps all through the city, they'd see a far more effective knockdown of the local beetle population.** Placing traps every 200 feet in town reduces local numbers substantially – it's certainly worth a try.

There's another problem with traps – each trap holds about 4,000 beetles. You're going to get way, way, WAY more than that. You are going to have to empty the traps daily.

Every day, dump the bags into a bucket of soapy water to drown the beetles. Then you can use the bags again. Don't use your everyday gloves to dump the bags, though, because these bugs stink like death. They will be all you smell, forever.

A good solution is to dump the dead beetles into the compost pile and cover them up. Add "brown" materials to balance out the "green" materials that the beetles will add to your compost.

Some people have rigged up the traps to make the beetles fall into a pan of water in the chicken yard. Make sure your chickens love these beetles before you do this. (Chickens can be weird – I used to have a few chickens who did not like earthworms. I don't know what was wrong with them.) Keep an eye on the chickens – sometimes they can fall out of love with a favorite food, and then your control method isn't as effective anymore, alas.

Traps actually are a good solution to the Japanese beetle problem, especially if you can get a bunch of neighbors in on the action, and if you combine traps with several other control methods.

Vacuuming

I would probably use a Shop-Vac to do this if you have a lot of beetles on a plant and are very frustrated. Plug it into a grounded outlet and start Hoovering the beetles off the leaves of your roses. You'll have to experiment with nozzle sizes, and how far to hold the nozzle from the leaves so you suck up beetles and not the entire plant.

Then once you have the beetles inside the Shop-Vac, quickly open the lid, tip in a glug of rubbing alcohol, then slam it shut before the beetles can fly out. Let the alcohol fumes knock down the beetles for about 5 minutes. After this, you should be able to open the Shop-Vac and not have beetles flying everywhere.

Dispose of the beetles in soapy water and get them out of the Shop-Vac, preferably in a shallow grave.

When I was taking my entomology class in college, we'd kill bugs for our collection by putting them in a Mason jar with a cotton ball soaked with rubbing alcohol. The alcohol fumes alone killed the insects. It's pretty effective.

Electric traps

In 1927 and 1928, some entomologists who were dreaming big went out and built the mother of all traps. These guys do not mess around. The first was a wooden frame with copper wires, each delivering 10,000 to 12,000 volts of death to each beetle that flew close enough to the wires to catch a spark.

The second trap was in the form of a three-foot hollow cube with peach branches sprayed with geraniol (an essential oil found in geranium plants) suspended in the middle as a lure.

An experimental trap, 3 feet square and 3 feet high, was constructed on a wooden frame with bare wire stretched in parallel strands on the sides and top. The alternate strands were connected so there would be a potential of 10,000 to 12,000 volts between any two adjacent strands. The trap was operated from a 110-volt, 60-cycle alternating current and consumed 0.13 to 0.18 kilowatt per hour, depending on the number of beetles touching the wires. Peach twigs sprayed with emulsified geraniol were suspended each day in the center of the trap to attract beetles.

Beetles were attracted at times from plants one-fourth mile away. Practically all coming into contact with the trap were killed. Less than 3 percent of the beetles collected on the ground near the trap were alive 48 hours later. The trap placed 4½ feet above the ground in a peach orchard electrocuted 592 beetles per hour. When it was elevated 9 feet above the ground, 935 beetles per hour were killed in the peach orchard and 857 per hour in an open field.

The use of the electrical trap made by Mehrhof and Van

"When [the trap] was elevated 9 feet above the ground, 935 beetles per hour were killed in the peach orchard and 857 per hour in an open field."

Now you can't sit there and read that and tell me that entomology is boring.

For obvious reasons, this 12,000 volt trap is not available on the market today, and I don't want any of my readers going out and building one. I just want you to know that entomologists are pretty awesome.

Cultural Control

Scientific studies suggest that beetles are attracted to plants that already have beetle damage.

If you have the patience to walk around your yard every evening, knocking beetles into a cup of water to feed them to your chickens, or if you keep spraying every evening, then you can keep the damage down to some extent. The beetles will still do a number on your roses and on the parts of your apple/elm/linden trees you can't reach from the ground. BUT in my experience, when I did this for a while, the numbers of beetles in my yard started to decline, even though it was still peak beetle season. **So, fewer beetles equals fewer pheromones equals fewer beetles coming in for a meal.**

Also, **withhold irrigating your lawn while the beetles are laying eggs.** The eggs need to absorb water to survive, and the newly-hatched grubs are vulnerable to dry conditions. Your lawn might look a little peaked, but once late August and early September rolls around, you can start irrigating again to help damaged turf recover from grub damage.

Use non-susceptible plants not subject to attack

If these beetles are driving you out of your gourd, you can get lists of non-susceptible plants from your state University Extension service. I did notice that Knock-Out roses seem to be not as plagued by beetles, but I need to look at other roses around the area to see if this is true elsewhere.

(Later note: It's true in some cases, but in other cases, heck yeah they get attacked. It's possible that native roses, such as *Rosa carolina* and *Rosa setigera*, are less affected by Japanese beetles. Would be glad to hear from readers about their experiences with Japanese beetles and native or antique roses.)

Plants subject to feeding by beetles [2]

Small fruits: Blackberry, blueberry, currant, grape,* raspberry,* strawberry.
Orchard fruits: Apple,* cherry,* nectarine, peach,* plum, quince.
Truck and garden crops: Asparagus, beans, rhubarb, sweet corn.*
Field crops: Alfalfa, clover, field corn,* soybean.
Ornamental shrubs and vines: Barberry, butterflybush, crapemyrtle, lespedeza, ornamental flowering cherry, rose,* shrub-althea,* Virginia creeper.
Ornamental garden plants: Canna, dahlia,* hollyhock,* marshmallow,* rose-mallow, snapdragon, zinnia.*
Shade trees: Elms, horsechestnut,* linden,* lombardy poplar,* Norway maple,* pin oak, planetree or buttonwood, white birch, willow.*

Plants rarely fed upon by beetles

Small fruits: Dewberry, gooseberry.
Orchard fruits: Pear.
Truck and garden crops: Cabbage, carrots, cauliflower, eggplant, lettuce, onion, parsley, pea, potato, radish, spinach, squash, sweetpotato, tomato, turnip.
Field crops: Barley, oats, rye, wheat.
Ornamental shrubs and vines: Azalea (except deciduous varieties), beautyberry, box, clematis, deutzia, English ivy, euonymus, evergreens, forsythia, honeysuckle, hydrangea, lilac, mockorange, privet, rhododendron, snowberry, spirea, weigela, wisteria.
Ornamental garden plants: Aquilegia, calendula, carnation, chrysanthemum, coreopsis, cosmos, four-o'clock, gladiolus, goldenglow, iris, larkspur, lily, nasturtium, pachysandra, pansy, peony, phlox, snapdragon, sweetpea, tulip, violet.
Shade trees: Ash, Carolina poplar, catalpa, dogwood, evergreens (except cypress), locust, maple (except Norway and Japanese), oaks (except pin and chestnut), redbud, sweetgum, tupelo, white poplar.

Extremely organic means of control

Fill a Super-Soaker water gun with soapy water and zap the beetles in your trees – though this might be more of a frustration thing here. Better yet, give your kids and their friends Super Soakers and a bucket of soapy water, and have them go outside and blast the beetles on your apple trees.

Or get a powerful sprayer, like a trombone sprayer, that reaches up into high branches, and use that to blast them with soapy water as the damned beetles fly out and go all over the place.

More effective, though, is to spray the beetles in the morning while it's still cool and they're moving slow, or in the cool of the evening once it starts getting dark. **Remember that Japanese beetles fly only in the daytime.** They're most active on warm, sunny days, and they prefer to feed on plants that are sitting in full sun. (This is why you don't see them as much in shady areas.)

When it's dark and cool, Japanese beetles are sitting ducks. If the weather is cool and the sun hasn't quite come up, lay a sheet under your afflicted tree, then shake the tree. The Japanese beetles should fall out onto the sheets. Then spray them with soapy water with a little rubbing alcohol added to kill them, and shake the tree again. Keep repeating until you've killed what beetles you can, then roll up the sheet and dispose of the bodies.

You could bury the little jerks just to get rid of the smell, but disposing of them in your hot compost pile would be a capital idea. Compost your beetles, improve your soil. At least you're getting some benefit from them.

Companion planting

Companion planting doesn't work so well when it comes to Japanese beetles. I've heard about some folks planting marigolds around their plants, trying to deter beetles – only to find the marigolds themselves swarming with Japanese beetles. One person just ended up pulling up his marigolds and shaking the beetles into a bag – he collected thousands of beetles that way.

Geraniums poison Japanese beetles

Annual geraniums (aka Pelargoniums) contains geraniol, which is an oil that attracts Japanese beetles. **But geraniums are also highly toxic to Japanese beetles.**

Thirty minutes after they eat the leaves, the beetles will roll over on their backs and lie paralyzed. They recover within 24 hours, unless some predator eats them up while they're lying immobilized. But older studies suggest that the geranium poison kills the beetle and destroys their digestive system. (Specifically, the poison in the geranium was recently identified as L-quisqualic acid, which targets neurotransmitters in the beetle's nervous system.)

You might even find the paralyzed beetles nestled on your geranium leaves. Knock them into your soapy water bucket, or call your little red hen over for a little snack.

Both zonal geraniums and ivy geraniums contain the chemical that paralyzes beetles. Plant 'em all!

Geraniol, an oil that is present in the geraniums and in other plants, is very effective in attracting the beetles. Some people spray geraniol on a tree or a bush to attract a bunch of beetles, then they spray the congregated beetles with poison. So, the geraniol attracts the beetles, and the L-quisqualic acid kills them.

An entomologist studying beetles and geraniums noted that **geraniums grown in the sun will kill many more beetles than those grown in the shade.** Also, the flowers of the geranium were much more poisonous than the leaves, though both do just fine in knocking down the beetles.

Throw out the roses, it's time to raise truckloads of geraniums!!

A couple of entomologists are trying to develop a botanical insecticide from these paralytic compounds. Stay tuned.

Entomophagy

Entomophagy simply means "eating insects," i.e. eating insects for lunch, supper, and for snacks!

If your initial reaction to this is ICK ICK ICK ICK, just skip this section to the next section, which involve essential oils and might be a little better for your nerves than this topic.

Japanese beetles are actually very good sources of food. Both beetles and grubs are edible, and up to 40 percent of their body weight is made up of protein.

To collect them, cut off the top of a 2-liter pop bottle, then take the cut-off part and invert it onto the base for an instant funnel. Then knock the beetles into this funnel.

Kill the beetles by freezing them for about 10 to 15 minutes. If you have only a few beetles, just leave them in the freezer until you get enough to cook up.

Some people simply fry the beetles in oil in a wok or a frying pan. Others boil the beetles for 15 minutes, then marinate them in a favorite sauce overnight (such as cranberry marinade). Then put them in the dehydrator and dry them to a crispy crunch.

It might take a little work to get past the ick factor, but hey, in a world where people eat haggis and deep-fried sticks of butter, I think we can stomach bugs, especially the apple-flavored bugs that have entirely devoured our apple trees in the backyard. And this form of revenge is particularly apt.

Essential oils

Field studies done with 41 different essential oils concluded that **wintergreen oil and peppermint oil were the two most effective oils at repelling Japanese beetles.** These oils were followed by **anise, bergamont mint, cedarleaf, dalmation sage, tarragon, and wormwood oil.**

Combining wintergreen oil with ginger, peppermint, or citronella oils also worked to mask the scent of desirable plants so the beetles couldn't smell them.

You can make your own cedar oil spray, if you can get your hands on some untreated Western red cedar planks.

Get 6 to 8 red Western cedar planks, each about four inches long, and set them in a five gallon bucket. (Actually, size doesn't matter here – they just need to be small enough to be submerged in the water in a five-gallon bucket.) Pour in enough hot water to cover them – use a teakettle of boiling water to bring up the heat – and let them sit in that for 24 hours. Put a brick on top of the cedar wood to keep it submerged.

Then strain out any loose particles, pour that water into your sprayer – don't dilute it – and spray it on the roses. You might have to try different numbers of planks, but when you have the strength right, the beetles will fall off the roses.

(Don't use Eastern red cedar on your food plants, because this variety of cedar can be poisonous. If you can't grill your food on it, skip it.)

These oils will need to be re-applied after every rain, and will also need to be sprayed about twice a week for the best benefit.

Essential oils are natural and also have the benefit of smelling good when you spray them. Think of it as aromatherapy for a beetle-stressed gardener.

Floating row covers
Floating row covers are specially designed fabrics that are laid over plants to protect them against frost. These can also keep insects and other pests out of your plants, including Japanese beetles.

As soon as the beetles show up in your yard, cover prized plants with floating row covers. Choose a light material that lets light in but doesn't trap much heat. Peg the edges of the cloth down securely so beetles can't wriggle their way in. Then use an organic insecticide to spray those little frustrated beetles that are trying to break in.

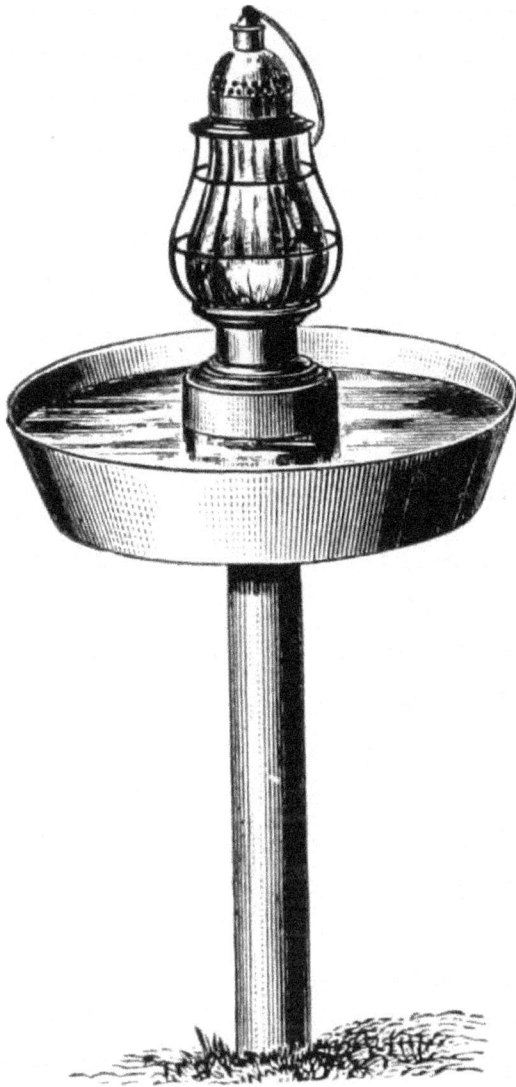

In the olden days, you'd make a beetle trap by putting a lantern in a small sea of kerosene. These were also the days when you'd spray arsenate of lead on your apples to kill insects. Talk about living dangerously.

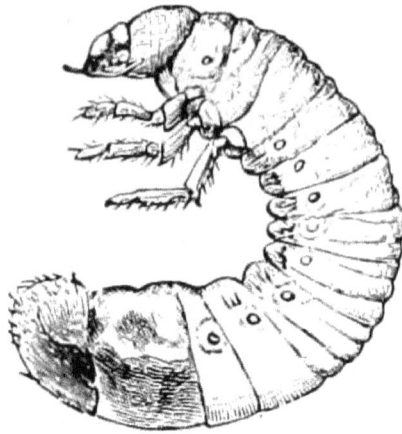

CONTROL OF WHITE GRUBS

Turf that has been afflicted by white grubs will take on a wilted appearance in April and May, and again in September and October, because those are when the old grubs (in spring) and the young grubs (in fall) are doing the bulk of their feeding on grass roots. Heavily infested grass can actually be rolled back, like a carpet, which sometimes reveal those grubs at their evil work. (When you do, have a bottle of insecticidal soap handy to spray those thin-skinned imps.)

The best way to manage grubs is to identify which grubs in your lawn are Japanese beetle grubs. There will be several kinds of grubs in your grass, but they're not all Japanese beetle grubs, but the Japanese beetle grubs will be your worst pest, and their life cycle is different from the life cycle of the other grubs. So, basically, the best way to target the Japanese beetles is to identify them, find out what their numbers are in your lawn, timing your pesticide application to target the Japanese beetle grubs, and then checking the treated area for results.

How to Scout for Grubs

Grubs live among the grass roots, chewing them off, which makes it harder for grass to take up enough water, especially when the weather is hot and dry. That's why you'll see a lot of big dead grass patches in grub-infested soil. You can even roll these section back, like a carpet, and see how the roots have been chewed away. By this time, the grubs have usually moved on to the next part of the all-you-can-eat buffet that is your lawn: the adjacent green part (which might not be looking as green any more).

Also, if you have a grub infestation, you might see starlings and crows digging up your grass to get at them. You might have moles digging through your yard to get at these tasty treats, with shrews and voles using the mole burrows to also get at the grubs. Or you might wake up in the morning to find a family of skunks digging for grubs in your yard, whereupon you turn right around and go right back to bed.

Identify different white grubs
– by checking out their posteriors.

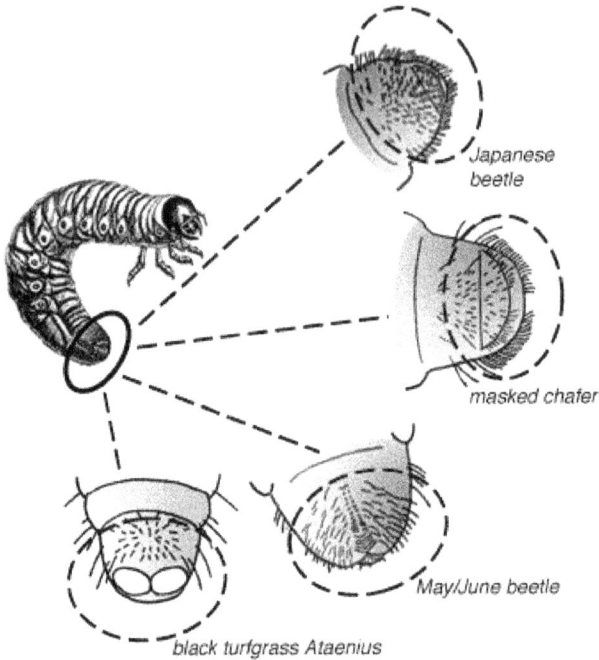

Japanese beetle

masked chafer

May/June beetle

black turfgrass Ataenius

(courtesy of the University of Minnesota Extension)

Tilling to Kill Grubs

Obviously, tilling your already-established yard is not going to work so well, but **tilling gardens will bring grubs to the surface where birds can get at them, and it decreases larval density in the tilled area by 72 percent.** Tilling, followed by planting a thick layer of cover crops, is one way that large-scale blueberry growers kept down local beetle populations. Studies found that cultivating in the spring and again in the fall reduced white grubs by 50 percent, then by 68 percent. So this is one natural way to keep grubs from getting established in fields.

If tilling is difficult, **cover crops (planted with non-grass species) also seems to keep the numbers of Japanese beetle larvae down.** The female beetles want to lay eggs in a big ol' patch of pristine lawn, not in some flower bed with all these *plants* in it.

Insecticides for Grubs

These work best when the grubs are close to the soil's surface and actively feeding. The first window of opportunity is in mid-spring until the grown beetles emerge in May. The second window is in late summer and early fall, after the eggs in the soil hatch and the young grubs start feeding.

Soil insecticides do not linger in the soil, so you'll need to apply them each season.

Two insecticides, imidacloprid and halofenozide, should be applied in early summer, June through mid-July.

Imidacloprid (Merit) is an insecticide made to mimic nicotine, which is also toxic to insects. Imidacloprid is a systemic, which means it's taken up through the roots of the plant and spreads through its leaves, stems, roots, fruits, and flowers. Imidacloprid is spread on turf from July until September to kill white grubs.

Note: Merit is terrible for honeybees and monarch butterflies and is often cited as being one of the causes of honeybee decline. Being a systemic, this insecticide will move up into blossoms – including clovers and apple blossoms – and kill the honeybees and butterflies that drink the nectar there.

Halofenozide should be used from July until the end of August, as it works best when the female beetles are still laying eggs. If you have trouble with thatch in your yard, you will get best results if you dethatch the yard before you apply it. This will allow the insecticide to penetrate better into the soil and mess up those female beetles that are trying to lay eggs in your dang lawn.

Endophytic Turfgrasses

These are just like regular turfgrasses, except these actually have a kind of fungus that lives inside the cells of the plants. The fungus and the grass share a symbiotic relationship – that is, the two different species have a relationship that benefits both. The fungus benefits because it has a safe place to live inside the grass cells, and the grass benefits because the fungus makes the grass taste bad to grazers, diseases, and pests.

So would endophyte-infected turfgrasses also taste bad to white grubs – and cause them to leave the grass alone?

The answer seems to be *maybe*. The endophytic grasses seem to be resistant to many foliage-feeding insect pests, and newer varieties of these grasses – specifically, **the turfgrasses that have been infected with** *Acremonium endophytes* **– seem to have developed more resistance to root-feeding white grubs.** Older varieties don't seem to have this resistance.

Cultivars with *Acremonium endophytes* include **'Reliant' and 'SR 3000' hard fescue,** *Festuca longifolia,* **'SR 5000,' and**

'Jamestown II' Chewings fescue.

Endophytes are mainly available in perennial ryegrass and fescue, but they're also trying to enhance other turfgrasses, such as Kentucky bluegrass, red fescue, and bentgrass with endophytes. The wheels of scientific inquiry turn incessantly.

Milky Spore Disease

Milky spore (*Paenibacillus popilliae*, formerly *Bacillus popilliae*) is a soil-dwelling bacterium that is responsible for a disease called milky spore that infects Japanese beetle grubs. This has been around for a while in the U.S. – it was the first insect pathogen to be registered in the United States as a microbial control agent.

When the grubs ingest the bacterium, the spores germinate in the grub's guts, then spreads to their blood (technically, the hemolymph) and multiplies. This causes the grub's body to turn a milky color (hence the name of the disease). Within 7 to 21 days, the grub dies, and then billions of new spores are released into the soil from its dead body.

Milky spore doesn't harm beneficial insects, birds, bees, or anything else besides grubs, and it survives in drought conditions.

Disadvantages include the high cost of production of the bacteria, as well as its slow rate of action. The milky spore bacteria has a harder time surviving in cold temperatures, so survival of this bacteria is not guaranteed in areas in Zone 5 and colder.

Milky spore works as a control method for grubs only,

and is not effective in decreasing the numbers of adult beetles in the area, because adult beetles tend to fly in from any old place up to two miles away. However, in the old days, there was a government program set up to spread milky spore disease over a large area. Between 1939 and 1953, over 100 tons of spore powder was applied to 160,000 sites in the U.S. This brought down the numbers of larvae in the turf, and this large-scale operation also brought down great numbers of adult beetles, and the beetle population stabilized at this lower rate.

These days, though, milky spore seems to be losing its killing edge against larvae.

August is the best time for inoculating the turf with milky spore, since the newly-hatched grubs are close to the surface of the soil and busily feeding on grass roots. (Also, in the insect world, young insects are more readily killed by diseases, while older ones have had time to toughen up.)

There are limitations to this approach. You can apply it in your yard, though that will not keep the beetles from coming in from everywhere else. Also, milky spore takes several years to become most effective, because what you are trying to do is inoculate the soil with bacterium. It takes several years to build up the population of the bacterium in the soil, so that's why you have to keep applying it every year. In general, you get the best results by spreading the milky spore inoculum over three years.

The best time to apply milky spore, or other larval treatments, is just after the beetles lay their eggs in early August – or when the grubs are still young in your area.

The problem with milky spore is that it doesn't seem to be as effective as it used to be. The grubs have been making a comeback in places where milky spore had worked in the past. Some field tests show that infected grubs are still busily eating grass roots just as uninfected grubs do. (At the same time, I'm curious if any field studies have been done to see if these infected grubs still pupate and hatch as healthy adults, or if the disease adversely affects the pupa and the adult beetle.) It's possible that some grubs might have developed immunity to the disease.

Milky spore disease should work in areas that haven't been infected with the Japanese beetle before, but it seems to have lost it effectiveness in areas where the infestation has been going on for a long time.

Spikes of Death

These were developed by a Colorado entomologist, Whitney Cranshaw. These are a particularly healthy and useful way to kill grubs, get some exercise, and aerate the lawn a little bit.

In April and May, and again in September and October, the grubs are feeding on grass roots within the top two inches of the ground. So Dr. Cranshaw came up with the killer idea (literally) to put a set of spikes on his shoes and go stomping around the yard, in an organized scientific way of course.

Basically, the spikes pierce the top layers of the grass roots where grubs are feeding, as well as the grubs themselves. This kills grubs and aerates the soil, which also is good for grass.

Using the Spikes o' Death takes some methodical walking – for best results, you'll have to walk over your yard three to five times in order to get two nail insertions per square inch. However, this methodical walking killed as many grubs as commonly used insecticides. Plus it's good exercise.

Spikes o' Death are usually sold as strap-on sandals through online garden supply companies.

Keep in mind that you won't be able to walk normally around your yard in these shoes, unless you want to break an ankle. You'll have some big spikes coming out of the bottoms of these, so take it slow.

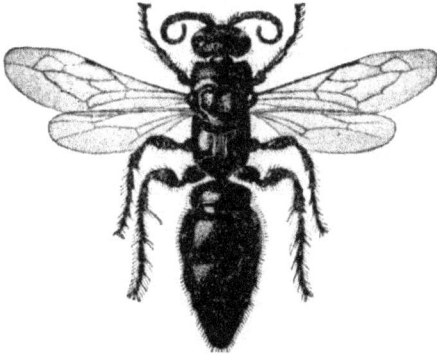

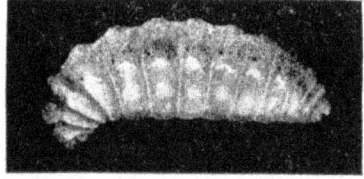

297

NATURAL PREDATORS, PARASITES, AND DISEASES

The Japanese beetle has a host of enemies in Japan. These enemies, along with the cool climate of the island and the scarcity of open grasslands, keep the beetle in check there.

Here in the United States, we have native predators, but not to the extent that we need to slow down beetle infestations. Birds seek out beetles; chickens snap them up; moles, shrews, and skunks love to snack on grubs. Their efforts have brought down the populations of grubs and beetles, and sometimes have even helped mitigate a local population of them. However, at this time, the pest is too widespread to be controlled by predators alone.

Insect parasites

Two insects provide biological control – the fly *Istocheta aldrichi*, and the tiphid wasp, *Tiphia vernalis*, though they don't have the large numbers necessary to control infestations.

In a scene straight out of a horror movie, certain kinds of wasps will lay eggs on Japanese beetle larvae, and when the eggs hatch, the wasp larvae feed on their hosts. Eek!

Entomopathogenic nematodes

These microscopic nematodes seek out grubs and other host insects in the soil. When a nematode finds a white grub, it gets inside of it. Now here is the gross part. These nematodes carry a bacterium in their gut. Once the nematode is inside the grub, it inoculates the grub with this bacteria, which quickly reproduces and grows inside the grub. The nematode eats the bacteria and *the nematode* reproduces. The grub dies of septicemia, and all those newly-grown nematodes head out into the world of the soil to find more grubs to infect.

The two nematodes which are the most effective against grubs are *Steinernema glaseri* and *Heterorhabditis bacteriophora*. Only the *H. bacteriophora* is available for sale at this time.

These nematodes are a little pricey, mainly because you're buying living creatures that need to be cared for. They need oxygen, and they can live for only a month or two under cool conditions. For best results, you must apply the nematode solution as soon as possible, and you must follow label directions, because it will do you absolutely no good to spray a bunch of dead nematodes on your yard. Read the storage directions and follow them to the letter – keep these nematode in a cool place and use them quickly.

When you're applying nematodes to your yard, follow the directions (usually you'll mix this solution with water). Use any standard insecticide applicator, but be sure to remove any screens before you put the nematode mixture in. On my old sprayer, I had a little screen at the bottom of the tank that led to the sprayer wand, and a second screen near the end of the wand. You have to unscrew certain parts of your sprayer to get to these. Applying the nematodes during a cloudy day is best, as the nematodes are sensitive to sunlight. Then, once you've sprayed them over your yard, water them in so they get into the soil and they don't dry out.

When you've finished and you're cleaning out your sprayer, be sure to put the screens back in!

THE TAKEAWAY

Whew. That was a lot of stuff about Japanese beetles but I hope that some of these ideas can help you reduce your infestation and help keep your plants healthy while those beetles are ravaging the world.

There are a number of takeaway points that can be applied to Japanese beetles, and any infestation.

1) Know thy enemy. Know what conditions they need to survive, and give them conditions in which they fail. Know what cultural practices they prefer, and deny those. Know what they eat, and find a way to keep them away from those food sources when possible.

2) Support plant health. Put organic material in the soil and mulch the plants. Feed the soil so the plant can build up its strength. This allows your plants to have an upper hand, or leaf, when they are undergoing an infestation.

3)   Fight the war on several different fronts. If you use a chemical control, use a cultural control at the same time, as well as hand-collection. Use several different means to target the insects for best results.

Good night, and good luck.

Please leave a honest review for this book on BookBub or Goodreads. Reviews are such a great help to the author, and I appreciate every review I receive. Thank you!

PREVIEWS OF MY OTHER GARDENING BOOKS

A sample of

Don't Throw in the Trowel: Vegetable Gardening Month by Month.

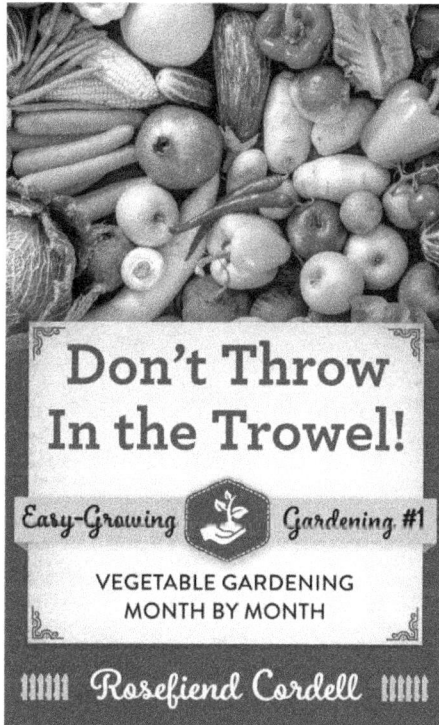

Chapter One

Save Time and Trouble With Garden Journals

When I worked as a municipal horticulturist, I took care of twelve high-maintenance gardens, and a number of smaller ones, over I-don't-know-how-many square miles of city, plus several hundred small trees, an insane number of shrubs, a greenhouse, and whatever else the bosses threw at me. I had to find a way to stay organized besides waking up at 3 a.m. to make extensive lists. My solution: keep a garden journal.

Vegetable gardeners with an organized journal can take control of production and yields. Whether you have a large garden or a small organic farm, it certainly helps to keep track of everything in order to beat the pests, make the most of your harvest, and keep up with spraying and fertilizing.

Keeping a garden journal reduces stress because your overtaxed brain won't have to carry around all those lists. It saves time by keeping you focused. Writing sharpens the mind, helps it to retain more information, and opens your eyes to the world around you.

My journal is a small five-section notebook, college ruled, and I leave it open to the page I'm working on at the time. The only drawback with a spiral notebook is that after a season or two I have to thumb through a lot of pages to find an earlier comment. A small three-ring binder with five separators would do the trick, too. If you wish, you can take out pages at the end of each season and file them in a master notebook.

I keep two notebooks – one for ornamentals and one for vegetables. However, you might prefer to pile everything into one notebook. Do what feels comfortable to you.

These are the five sections I divide my notebooks into – though you might use different classifications, or put them in different orders. Don't sweat it; this ain't brain surgery. Feel free to experiment. You'll eventually settle into the form that suits you best.

First section: To-do lists.

This is pretty self-explanatory: you write a list, you cross off almost everything on it, you make a new list.

When I worked as horticulturist, I did these lists every month. I'd visit all the gardens I took care of. After looking at anything left unfinished on the previous month's list, and looking at the garden to see what else needed to be done, I made a new, comprehensive list.

Use one page of the to-do section for reminders of things you need to do next season. If it's summer, and you think of some chores you'll need to do this fall, make a FALL page and write them down. Doing this has saved me lots of headaches.

Second section: Reference lists.

These are lists that you'll refer back to on occasion.

For example, I'd keep a list of all the yews in the parks system that needed trimmed, a list of all gardens that needed weekly waterings, a list of all places that needed sprayed for bagworms, a list of all the roses that needed to be babied, etc.

I would also keep my running lists in this section, too – lists I keep adding to.

For instance, I kept a list of when different vegetables were ready for harvest – even vegetables I didn't grow, as my friends and relatives reported to me. Then when I made a plan for my veggie garden, I would look at the list to get an idea of when these plants finished up, and then I could figure out when I could take them out and put in a new crop. I also had a list of "seed-to-harvest" times, so I could give each crop enough time to make the harvest date before frost.

You can also keep a wish list – plants and vegetables you'd like to have in your garden.

Third section: Tracking progress.

This is a weekly (or, "whenever it occurs to me to write about it") section as well.

If you plant seeds in a greenhouse, keep track of what seeds you order, when you plant them, when they germinate, how many plants you transplant (and how many survive to maturity), and so forth.

When you finish up in the greenhouse, use these pages to look back and record your thoughts – "I will never again try to start vinca from seeds! Never!! Never!!!" Then you don't annoy yourself by forgetting and buying vinca seeds next year.

You can do the same thing when you move on to the vegetable garden – what dates you tilled the ground, planted the seeds, when they germinated, and so forth. Make notes on yields and how everything tasted. "The yellow crooknecks were definitely not what I'd hoped for. Try yellow zucchini next year."

Be sure to write a vegetable garden overview at season's

end, too. "Next year, for goodness' sake, get some 8-foot poles for the beans! Also, drive the poles deeper into the ground so they don't fall over during thunderstorms."

During the winter, you can look back on this section and see ways you can improve your yields and harvest ("The dehydrator worked great on the apples!"), and you can see which of your experiments worked.

Fourth section: Details of the natural world.

When keeping a journal, don't limit yourself to what's going on in your garden. Track events in the natural world, too. Write down when the poplars start shedding cotton or when the Queen's Anne Lace blooms.

You've heard old gardening maxims such as "plant corn when oak leaves are the size of a squirrel's ear," or "prune roses when the forsythia blooms." If the spring has been especially cold and everything's behind, you can rely on nature's cues instead of a calendar when planting or preventing disease outbreaks.

Also, by setting down specific events, you can look at the journal later and say, "Oh, I can expect little caterpillars to attack the indigo plant when the Johnson's Blue geranium is blooming." Then next year, when you notice the buds on your geraniums, you can seek out the caterpillar eggs and squish them before they hatch. An ounce of prevention, see?

When I read back over this section of the journal, patterns start to emerge. I noticed that Stargazer lilies bloom just as the major heat begins. This is no mere coincidence: It's happened for the last three years! So now when I see the large buds, I give the air conditioner a quick checkup.

Fifth section: Notes and comments.

This is more like the journal that most people think of as being a journal – here, you just talk about the garden, mull over how things are looking, or grouse about those supposedly blight-resistant tomatoes that decided to be contrary and keel over from blight.

I generally put a date on each entry, then ramble on about any old thing. You can write a description of the garden at sunset, sketch your peppers, or keep track of the habits of bugs you see crawling around in the plants. This ain't art, this is just fun stuff (which, in the end, yields great dividends).

Maybe you've been to a garden talk on the habits of Asian melons and you need a place to put your notes. Put them here!

This is a good place to put garden plans, too. Years later I run into them again, see old mistakes I've made, and remember neat ideas I haven't tried yet.

Get a calendar.

Then, when December comes, get next year's calendar and the gardening journal and sit down at the kitchen table. Using last year's notes, mark on the calendar events to watch out for -- when the tomatoes first ripen, when the summer heat starts to break, and when you expect certain insects to attack. In the upcoming year, you just look at the calendar and say, "Well, the squash bugs will be hatching soon," so you put on your garden gloves and start smashing the little rafts of red eggs on the plants.

A garden journal can be a fount of information, a source of memories, and most of all, a way to keep organized. Who thought a little spiral notebook could do so much?

If you enjoy this book, grab a copy!

Now a sample chapter from my book on roses:
Rose to the Occasion: An Easy-Growing Guide to Rose Gardening.

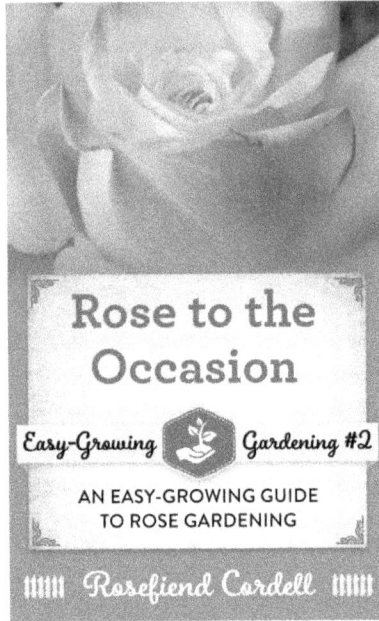

Roses are the Queen of Flowers. They're beautiful, fragrant, and elegant - and roses require all the pampering of a real Queen, don't they?

Actually, they don't!

Rose gardening can be easy and pleasant. I've worked 25 years in horticulture and cared for over 300 roses in a public rose garden when I was municipal horticulturist. I found ways to keep rose gardening fussbudgetry to a minimum while growing vigorous roses that bloomed their heads off. Rose to the Occasion: An Easy-Growing Guide to Rose Gardening shares tricks and shortcuts that rosarians use, plus simple ways you can keep up with your to-do list in the rose garden.

Gardeners of all skill levels will find this book helpful, whether they be beginning gardeners or old rosarians, whether they have a green thumb or a brown thumb.

Rose to the Occasion is the ultimate resource for any rose gardener, or anybody in need of good gardening advice. Roses are filled with romance, history, color, and fragrance. Grow some. They are worth it.

INTRODUCTION

When I started working as city horticulturist, I took care of a bunch of gardens around the city, including the big Krug Park rose garden. It included a bunch of the usual scrawny tea roses, some shrub roses, and a bunch of bare ground.

At the time I was more of a perennials gal, but when I looked at the roses, some of them were really nice. The 'Carefree Delight' roses were covered with rumpled pink blossoms. There was a tall 'Mr. Lincoln' rose and some 'Double Delights' that smelled amazing. A bunch of 'Scarlet Meidilands' were really putting on a blooming show, with tiny scarlet flowers cascading all over them. Not shabby at all.

I started taking care of the roses, but I noticed that a lot of the 'Scarlet Meidilands' were sprouting odd growths. Most of the new growth looked fine, with bronzed, flat leaves that looked attractive. But some of the new growth was markedly different – skinny, stunted leaves with pebbled surfaces, and hyperthorny canes that were downright rubbery. The blossoms on these shoots were crinkled and didn't open worth a darn.

I hollered at Charles Anctil, a Master Rosarian with the American Rose Society. We'd known each other since 1992 when we both worked at the Old Mill Nursery. He'd been working with roses for a good 50 years, and he knows his stuff. At any rate, Charles looked over the roses and told me that those roses, and others, had rose rosette virus, a highly contagious disease, and a death sentence for a rose. Every one of those roses had to come out. He couldn't believe the extent of the damage. He said that he had never seen so many roses infected by rose rosette in one place.

Oh great! Why do I get to be the lucky one?

I dug up many roses that spring. That winter, I got a work crew and dug up 50 more. I had to replace all those roses, so I started researching new varieties.

As city horticulturist with no staff, I was already running like hell everywhere I went, so I wanted roses that wouldn't wilt or croak or wrap themselves in blackspot every time I looked at them cross-eyed. I wanted tough roses, roses that took heat and drought and bug attacks and zombie apocalypses with aplomb and would still come out looking great and covered with scented blossoms. (And the blossoms HAD to be scented – there was no two ways about that.)

I started reading rose catalogs. I talked to Charles some more, which is always fun. Somewhere along the way, I got obsessed. I immersed myself in roses. That's how I learn – I get excited about a subject and start reading everything in sight about it, as if it's a mini-course in school. I read about antique roses, which were making a comeback. Different rose breeders, most notably David Austin, were crossing modern varieties with old varieties and to get roses that combined the best of the new and the old. Other breeders were creating roses that were tough and disease-resistant, such as the 'Knock-Out' landscape rose, which now you see everywhere.

I planted some antique roses, and they looked great. I planted more. The rose garden was starting to look spiffy, even though I still had to take roses out every year due to the rose rosette virus. I even tucked in some annuals and perennials around the garden to doll up the place when the roses conked out in July and August.

Roses are amazing plants. Many old roses have a long and storied history. Some species that were growing during the time of the Pyramids are still blooming today. And these roses are attractive and fragrant. What could be better?

Some people say that you can't grow roses organically. I say you can. I did use a few chemicals when I was a horticulturist, but that was because I had a huge list of things to do in a limited amount of time. I used Round Up for spot-weeding (a tiny squirt for each weed, just enough to wet the leaves), a systemic granular fungicide to keep up with blackspot, and Miracle-Gro as part of the fertilizing regimen for convenience.

If you choose to use chemicals, use them responsibly. Don't spray them and expect the problem to be fixed. They work best when you combine them with other control methods. I'll give you an example that's not rose-related. I had a mandevilla plant in the greenhouse that had a huge mealybug problem. (Mealybugs are a small, white insect that sucks out plant juices. The young bugs look like bits of cotton.) I sprayed the plant with insecticide until the leaves were dripping. The mealybugs were still there. I put a systemic insecticide around the roots of the plant and watered it in. The mealybugs didn't care.

So I just started squishing the mealybugs with my fingers, a gross job because they squirt orange goo. At that point, I didn't care. I searched them out and squashed them where they were cuddled up around buds, in the cracks of the plant, and under the leaves. I even found some on the roots just under the soil. I squished those and added a little extra potting soil. I checked the plant every other day and squished every mealybug I could find. After a while, I stopped finding them altogether. Then I fertilized the plant, and the mandevilla put out leaves like crazy and started blooming. Success!

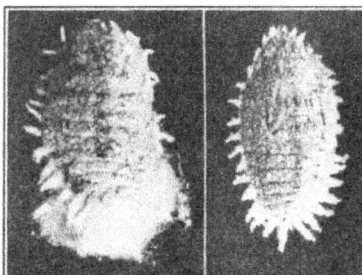

Chemicals aren't a cure-all by any means. They're convenient, but sometimes you just have to get in and do a little hands-on work with the plant to help it along. It's a good feeling when a plant you've been working with rights itself and perks up again.

Though I'm no longer a horticulturist, I wrote this book because I have worked in horticulture for about half my life, and have a decent understanding about how the natural world works. I might possibly be just a little crazy about roses. I hope my experiences are helpful and that you're able to benefit from them – and that your roses benefit as well.

The end of the sample!!

Get a copy of <u>Rose to the Occasion</u> today.

Leave Me A Lawn: Lawn Care for Tired Gardeners

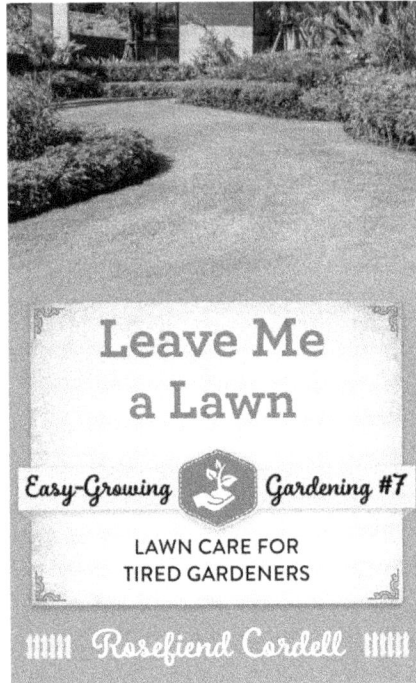

How do I make my lawn look like a golf course without using all those chemicals? How do I keep up with all the lawn care when I have a million things to do?

Leave Me A Lawn is packed with clear, concise information on yard care that is written with a sense of humor and a lot of helpful information on lawn maintenance from a former horticulturist with a trick back. Discover time-saving secrets for better fertilizing, watering and mowing, and helpful hints for those of you who already have too much on your plate.

This book also contains advice for those lawn maniacs out there who want that green, lush grass but want to cut back on chemicals and water. You can grow lean and mean grass that fights off insect pests and diseases, and take drought with aplomb.

Planting a Gorgeous Lawn

Of course, your climate and your soil will affect your grass choices, as well as planting times.

Cool-season grasses should be planted in late summer or early fall. This time of year, the soil is nice and warm, which aids in germination, and any annual weeds that come up with the grass are killed off by frost. Not only that, but the grass has three seasons to get established -- fall, winter, and spring – before summer's heat and drought strike. Then you don't have to constantly water the grass as you would have if the grass had been planted in spring.

(P.S. Winter does count as a growing season. In all but the very coldest days of winter, roots are quietly growing underground, even when the soil is frozen.)

Be sure to sow your fall seeds at least four weeks before the first frost date. Six weeks before the first frost is best, so they can get their root system growing.

Warm-season grasses, on the other hand, are best planted in spring so they can luxuriate in the delicious summer heat before that awful cold sets in.

Now, sometimes you have no choice but to plant at some other time of year. I've heard that you can plant seed even in winter, throwing it on the snow cover (which would be great for even coverage – the snow would show up any gaps in your sowing). The seeds melt down with the snow, not germinating, and they get cuddled in with the ground very well for early spring, then they grow when they're ready.

And you can still plant grass in spring or even in summer (if you're able to keep up with keeping it watered) if you need to.

Really, if you can work with the plants – that is, keep them watered, or throw a little straw over them to protect them from the harsh summer sun – then you should be fine. Plants are really forgiving, when it comes to it. And if some of the grass seedlings die off for some reason, it's still okay. Just re-seed the bare patches later.

When you're dealing with living things, whether it be with plants, animals, or even humans (*cough*kids!*cough*), sometimes they turn out to be contrary, stubborn, bull-headed, or goofballs, and they don't act the way you want them to. That's the way it goes. Just try again later.

Seeding the lawn

Generally, grass seed should be sown at about 3 pounds per 1,000 square feet – but each mix and variety will differ, so check the package for the recommended amount.

April and May are the best months for seeding the lawn, but you can do it most any month where you get a decent amount of rainfall, or any time you're able to keep the lawn watered. I've seen good effects from seeding in the bleak midwinter, on top of snow. Obviously you can't take the seeder out when there's snow on the ground, but if you hand-sow, you can see where the seed falls and then add in more. (If you go this route, seed before a big snowstorm comes in so it gets covered up so the birds don't eat it.)

Personally, if I had a big construction area that needed to be seeded, I would seed everything in white clover and let it fix nitrogen into the soil. Then, the next spring, I'd kill it off with some broadleaf herbicide and put down grass seed. Annnnnnnd this is why I will never live anywhere there's a Homeowner's Association, because they'd probably run me out of town on a rail.

Maybe I should call this book the Redneck's Guide to Lawns. Well, actually no, because I know a lot of rednecks and we just don't do lawns ... because we need someplace to drive the four-wheeler. Next!

(I really shouldn't joke about rednecks because they're all armed.)

But seriously, if you're in a place where you *don't* have neighbors or HOAs that tell you what you need to put in your lawn, plant white clover to put nitrogen into the soil. Leave it in until it's time to reseed, then kill it off with broadleaf herbicide, or, for organic folks, use industrial-strength vinegar. (If you use industrial-strength vinegar, be sure to wear gloves and goggles. This is much, much more acidic than the vinegar you put on your salad, and I guarantee it will burn you. It's a good herbicide, though. So use with caution.)

After you kill off the clover, mow off the dead clover at the lawnmower's lowest setting, then leave the rest there as a mulch. Then reseed the yard with grass seed, raking in the seed when you're done.

You might have to use broadleaf herbicide on any

remaining patches of clover a couple of times to kill it off, or spot-spray rogue patches. At any rate, the nitrogen that the clover will add to your yard is valuable. The clover roots help hold the soil in place, and keep nitrogen in the yard for a little while longer, and add humus to the soil as they decay. (Humus is organic material, and necessary to keep soil abuzz with life, which in turn helps invigorate your grass roots in a million ways.)

Also, that nitrogen is the element that you want in your yard for your grass. Nitrogen is what makes grass lush and green. And to have that nitrogen actually below the soil's surface, naturally, instead of through some chemical fertilizer on top of the soil, is very effective, because it's right at root level where the grass roots need it most.

Grab a copy of <u>Leave Me a Lawn</u> today!

Me in 1995, when I embarked upon the grand adventure
of being a published author.
I was kind of a writing hotshot back then.
If you want to be perfectly honest, I still am.

ABOUT THE AUTHOR

I've worked in most all aspects of horticulture – garden centers, wholesale greenhouses, as a landscape designer, and finally as city horticulturist, where I took care of 20+ gardens around the city. I live in northwest Missouri with my husband and kids, the best little family that ever walked the earth. In 2012, when I was hugely pregnant, I graduated from Hamline University with a master's of writing for children; three weeks later, I had a son. It was quite a time.

My first book, **Courageous Women of the Civil War: Soldiers, Spies, Medics, and More** was published by Chicago Review Press in August 2016. This is a series of profiles of women who fought or cared for the wounded during the Civil War.

I've been sending novels out to publishers and agents since 1995, and have racked up I don't know how many hundreds of rejections. I kept getting very close – but not close enough. Agents kept saying, "You're a very good writer, you have an excellent grasp of craft, but I just don't feel that 'spark'...." Even after *Courageous Women* was published, they still weren't interested in my books.

In September 2016, I rage-quit traditional publishing and started self-publishing, because I wanted to get my books out to people who *would* feel that 'spark.' In my first year, I published 15 books. At this moment, I'm up to 29. (When you've been writing novels for over 20 years, you're going to have a bit of a backlog.) I am working at all these books and having a complete blast. I love doing cover work and designing the book interiors. I work full-time as a proofreader, so I handle that in my books as well.

And now I'm finding fans of my books who do feel that 'spark.' They're peaches, every one of them.

I'm finally doing what I was put on this earth to do.

There's no better feeling than that.

If you like this book, please leave a review on my BookBub or Goodreads page. Reviews help me get more readers.

Thanks so much for reading!
melindacordell.com

www.ingramcontent.com/pod-product-compliance
Lightning Source LLC
Chambersburg PA
CBHW032055040426
42335CB00037B/815